THERE CAME DOWN A NIGHTINGALE AND OTHER POEMS

SRIDEV MOHAN

ISBN 979-888569521-3

To my dear World...

Contents

Foreword

A poet is a man speaking to men, endowed with a more lively sensibility, as stated by William Wordsworth. It is true and at the same time he is a better human being than ordinary men and of course different from other human beings.

A poet is always unique and extraordinary. He sees and feels differently... and think, imagine and write distinctly. Here is a poet, who is blessed with this unique sensibility, imagination and thoughts. Sridev Mohan, through this collection of poems makes his humble but distinct contribution to English poetry.

This collection contains twenty short poems and a long poem. All the poems in this anthology, though different in theme, turn complementary to each other by the common concerns and considerations of the times. All these poems are reflections about the past, reasoning about the present and hopes for a better future. Viewing earth and life from an eco-aesthetic perspective, the poet becomes prophetic and warns humanity about the consequences that may follow, if we do not stop committing atrocities against nature. The last poem is a beautiful mythical-mystical verse that speaks beautifully against the brutality that man is showing against nature.

This collection also has under currents of the international intrigues and political agenda behind issues that have culminated in dangers like global warming, communal discriminations, and racial antagonisms etc. Through the narration of the tale of Odatious and

Preshious, by Grandmother Peace to the grandchildren, the poet is giving a green message to posterity. It creates hopes about a green future through the mystical meteors in the firmament that reaffirms and reiterates our commitment to Mother Earth.

These poems are decked with the altruistic hues of love and compassion. The poet dreams about and speaks for a better and safer future, not for his own generation only but for all generations to be born. These poems envisage a millennium beyond the barriers of caste, creed and race:

"All done for tomorrow,
Which we may never see.
Space is the only way
To no religion, bias or creed."

Through a laconic poetic style, the poet is eloquently and elegantly vouching for an egalitarian and exemplary world. He becomes distressed by frenzy and fury all around and through the sleep of the baby child, he is depicting the inner goodness and tranquility that each of us crave for. It also portrays how these are destroyed by the mad pursuit of life about. Sridev's poems often turn proverbial:

"Time is like perfume
Good when craved
Better when used
It is what we consume."

This poem end with a reflection about transience, mysteriousness and uncertainties of life. The poet realizes that it is impossible to know a person fully. However much we may try to know, there still remains more to be known. Speaking about a person who exits the stage of life, he writes: "We knew that person. But now no more."

The same philosophical reflections can be traced in another poem: "In all we are a bunch of gases… In you and me resides the answer to this race." The poem that is addressed to a nightingale, reminds us of Keats, Shelley and definitely the poetic sensibility of the entire Romantic Age. The poet is asking for "Wings to fly… I found reasons to live, hug and share." Surely, these poems elicit the exquisite nuances of genuine poetic talent and stylistic novelty.

Congratulations and best wishes to my dear friend Sridev Mohan. May more of your writings come to us and illumine our ways of thinking and action.

Dr. Milon Franz

Professor and Research Guide

Department of English

St Xavier's College for Women, Aluva

Kerala

Preface

I still remember the colossal impact the poem 'The Jaguar' by Ted Hughes had on me the first time I read it. That was some time ago. But that massive literary and spiritual shock still lingers within quite strongly and will stick with me till the very end. Several people, films and books have helped me in shaping the self, the thoughts, and the very core of my existence. But it should be professed without a second's doubt that this one poem equals all those other literary outputs and human lives combined. Why? Doesn't matter. A piece of literature strikes the readers' minds, individually. Hughes' Jaguar, still residing in that cage, yet with fiery eyes and unbound energy, shapes into the role model so necessary for the current age. That poem holds a special position in my pantheon of role models…

The Jaguar, as a mode of inspiration and a benchmark of literary achievement had taken hold of me almost six years back. There then commenced a slow burning desire to publish a book of poems written by myself sometime in the future. That foundation was laid in 2018 when I began this project (though initially I had no intention of saving the poem for later use) with a poem describing the Fifa World Cup happening in Russia. And through the last three years, I like to think that I made a start for a long odyssey that is beckoning me to poetic shores afar. Twenty one poems form the content of this literary work which definitely is a request to humanity to simply live. I do not wish to expound more on what each poem holds, though I must say the poems range from discussing space, religion, passion, war, internal thoughts, humour etc. The rest can be figured by the reader (let the Jaguar do its job).

I have known Dr Milon Franz for over nine years now. I have had the pleasure to have read her poems, all thought provoking pieces of literature in verse. And so, when I felt that the time had come for stepping ahead with publishing this book of poems, there was only her name in mind for writing a foreword to my book. A beautiful human to begin with, then a well accomplished academician and a prolific writer of books and scholarly articles, along with a host of administrative affairs to deal with as part of her professional life, Dr Milon took time to painstakingly go through all the poems and share with me what she found was commonly passing through them, which I personally missed out to notice. And there I knew that she was the perfect person to write a note on my poems. I thank you Dr Milon for having shared your valuable words for this maiden project. I need to thank several literary stalwarts for having spurred my imagination while a student and later on while teaching in class. To mention just a few would include John Milton, William Blake, Nissim Ezekiel and Madhavikutty. I would like to thank Notion Press for helping with the publication of this book. I thank my wife, my friends and my family for inspiring me with ideas. I finally thank my imagination for helping in selecting those particular ideas that have turned into screenplays, short stories or as here, into poems.

Sridev Mohan

16/01/2022

1. Poem One

Everything will be round,
For thirty days from today.
All eyes will roll into one,
And see the goalposts sway.
Here comes the sport,
The biggest event on earth.
For legions of fans shall
Rejoice, for there's no dearth.
This ninety minute game
Can teach you to tackle life.
It'll equip you with stamina,
Spirit and a mind without rife.
So watch the World Cup from
Anywhere and see how,
And why humanity is going
To Russia with lots of love.
(This poem was written during the Fifa World Cup 2018 held in Russia.)

2. Poem Two

Do you see that light,
Straight ahead?
Do you want it,
Or will just sleep instead?
Is it not time to get up,
And move forward?
Is it not time to wash away
Yesterday and now be heard?
Run or walk or crawl said
Martin Luther King Jr.
But you gotta keep
Moving, moving and moving.
Good morning folks,
As I write my new lay.
Wake up and think about life,
Because right now it's Sunday.

3. Poem Three

Many a million mile
Has Voyager 1 gone.
Away from humanity,
Still brisk and agile.
Many a step have we
Placed to better yesterday.
All done for tomorrow,
Which we may never see.
Space is the only way
To no religion, bias or creed.
There abounds silence,
And galaxies happy and gay.
On earth laws make sense
To those who disrupt it.
And the rest will cry and fret
Over the loss of innocence.

4. Poem Four

Tiny and so very cute,
Is our baby child.
Didn't sleep yesterday,
Cried on and on, never mute.
Baby wasn't hungry,
Or in any other pain.
The fan was working,
But baby was still angry.
Baby was handed to all,
Like in a baton race.
Till morning none of us slept,
And baby finally snored in the hall.
In silence at last we smiled,
And closed our eyes.
And then a loud bike roared by,
And baby began, now so very wild.

5. Poem Five

They have been here,
Way before life came.
They will stay long after,
Life dies in shame.
They are a curse
And a blessing.
They have powers
Beyond our guessing.
We can proclaim success,
But the heat will tear us.
We can command technology,
But the water will flood us.
So, in front of the sun and rain,
We are a tiny bit.
The sun that warms life,
And the rain that cools it.

6. Poem Six

Time is like perfume.
Good when craved.
Better when used.
It is what we consume.
So, shall you be heard?
Do tell me now.
And about the future.
Will you be remembered?
We spit out wars.
Practise ill thoughts.
Forget the actions.
Echoing back in roars.
Once, we'll leave this shore.
And people shall gather.
They'll say, "We knew that person.
But now no more."

7. Poem Seven

Sat i on a chair.
Brooding about boredom.
Came along a mosquito.
And i lost my freedom.
He hovered near and far.
Oh he's so dumb.
Escaped he from my hands.
And made it for my cheek.
Haha!! The idiotic insect.
Indeed he is a geek.
I hit so hard on his body.
Strong hands, not weak.
He easily flew away.
While i broke my teeth.

8. Poem Eight

In all
We are
A bunch
Of gases.
In as
Much as
We can see
Powers to ashes.
In us
We see
The stars
And space.
In you
And me
Resides the
Answer to this race.

9. Poem Nine

He woke up again.
Though foolish man,
Put *Him* in pain.
That's called trust.
In your own ability,
Which should come first.
He knew who *He* was.
So *He* used *His* divinity,
Not for gain or loss.
But man is always the outsmarted.
So he showed off and,
Put *Him* down and down.
Well, *He* waited, without disdain.
And when man thought he won,
He woke up again.

10. Poem Ten

Lean against the sky,
And catch the wind.
Run among the clouds,
And live unsinned.
Grow trees and flowers,
Where there is no land.
Build walls and cities,
Without a plan and a hand.
Its then that you breathe,
While you start to live.
Its then that you fight,
To smile and give.

11. Poem Eleven

Cold 'n crispy,
Celebrations all filthy.
Sacrifice taught,
Jealousy learnt.
That *He* gave *his life*,
For a trillion idiots in strife.
This is what loving Jesus,
Should make us wish Merry Christmas.

12. Poem Twelve

There came down a nightingale,
Perched on my window, so very frail.
The scary wind was dancing wild.
So I cuddled the bird like my child.
Life in jail was damn too bad.
But I would still laugh, and then be sad.
Thirty years I got for with a gun,
I ended the life of a loving mother's son.
No one knew I could love, not even me.
But this l'il bird, I felt, could see
How a ruffian of massive built
Could hold it with a smile and head's slight tilt.
My nightingale, thus gave me wings to fly,
And I soared, in that four walled room, so high.
There, in those moments of joy and care,
I found reasons to live, hug and share.

13. Poem Thirteen

Next to the evening wind and sun
Sat I with a closed book.
The words in print weren't fun
As my brain stopped, oh the ol'crook.
I started to blame that organ
For it was now totally of no use.
Not to mention all the exams where
I failed, as it plucked its own fuse.
And so I decided to ruminate
On the world and its days.
Then my eyes saw my body weight
From no work and sweat and lazy ways.
That's when I felt my brain
Become heavy and sad.
Though my mind was like a Great Dane
T'was making my body bad.

14. Poem Fourteen

Whoosh! Here we go!
Speeding with light.
And ready for a show,
That's space's vast night.
Each light-year gone,
Smaller turns our home.
Turn back then, see all known,
Our dead dears, Indus and Rome.
Witness inventions, every age,
That we all learnt in class.
Ooooh! The Bard and his stage,
And now Pangea the land mass.
Our eyes just roll and pop,
Witnessing water bearing life.
5 billion years on we turn and stop,
To see no Earth, no humans and no strife.

15. Poem Fifteen

I woke up and strolled out.
Numerous lives walked about.
Footwear prints on the dusty way.
I stood confused on that bright day.
Wear I did my old magic shoes.
That helps me tread a life I choose.
Those million footprints stared at me.
Onto which print to step on I had to see.
I first opted on a zig zag pattern.
Those were of a drunkard so western.
Next I became an old corrupt politician.
Then a dog, beggar, priest and musician.
From each life to life like that I went.
Doomed eternally not to be permanent.
Because, a rain rained on that path so dusty.
And I, now a sweeper, brushed away my reality.

16. Poem Sixteen

Innocent i am says people.
So caring and loving.
Foolish but not demeaning.
A true devotee going to temple.
No harmful thoughts i think.
Nor do i crave for positions.
Always calm and no tensions.
Malice being washed down the sink.
The perfect person, an epitome.
The brightest star among a cluster.
The best soul, a truster.
The lovable guest at every home.
But now i declare in your presence.
I'm a greedy destroyer of Earth.
And continue that, i'll in mirth.
The top twelve lines is thus, repentance.

17. Poem Seventeen

Try to stay away from food to eat.
Try to find love in the sweltering heat.
Try to stop being so pretentious.
Try to feel each moment as auspicious.
Try to cry even if you got a six pack.
Try to sleep one day in a leaky shack.
Try to see death when you dig for gold.
Try to curb desires before your soul is sold.
Try to be happy in your own downfalls.
Try to gossip against thyself behind the walls.
Try to show off when no one is watching.
Try to pray even while you are washing.
Try to stop thinking independence is cool.
Try to see that to just sit you need a floor or stool.
Try to love being weak sometime.
Try to see that being soft isn't a major crime.

18. Poem Eighteen

A scary storm came by,
On the way where I stood.
The storm said 'hi',
In the best way it could.
The storm was quite fast,
As it took me in its arms.
The storm swept past
Dwellings, schools and farms.
The storm and I flew,
Over vast seas and lands.
The storm and I grew,
Into friends with no demands.
The storm kept me cosy,
And we danced along.
The storm became blowsy,
And rough became the song.
The storm became an addiction,
Slowly, mildly and softly.
The storm caused a sensation,
In me quite powerfully.
The storm began to weaken,
As I took the reins.
The storm now was taken,

And I locked it in chains.
The storm wreaked havoc,
Through the evil in me.
The storm was my luck,
To take revenge with a glee.
The storm begged a lot,
Asking me to stop.
The storm was caught,
By me like a knop.
The storm yelled,
Seeing all that I levelled.
The storm got quelled,
As I revelled.

19. Poem Nineteen

So come my pal and let us walk to the shore.
Let us witness the waves wet the sandy floor.
There are people and birds and the sun above.
See a father caress his child with tender love.
The water is washing our feet, so gentle and kind,
As deep and heavy thoughts now rush to the mind.
Was it here that life first moved onto land?
Will we ever find that footprint on this sand?
Just wonder how great it was for life to form,
And then be washed away, which is the norm.
All bad and good will thus be wiped off.
There will be time no more for a smile or scoff.
Yet eons back on this coastline was history made.
And here we stand with a chance before we fade.
So come my pal and we'll walk away from the shore.
Achieving footprints on the wet sandy floor.

20. Poem Twenty

Now dear, the time has come.
When in the sky the stars have risen.
Now as a change dawns in the season,
When still, a lone ant carries a bread crumb.
Now dear, the time has come,
When the sickness races through the blood.
Now must we kneel and pray in the mud,
When a cat and a mouse runs into a drum.
Now dear, the time has come.
When we both can simply love one another.
Now as Earth switches off her bright brother.
When the tiny spider casts its next home.
Now dear, the time has come,
When we can have passion like a storm.
Now as that raw love rushes through the corm.
When the cosmic time is 'now', the total sum.

21. Poem Twenty One

To all the children running and gliding
Around the village ground, spoke out
Grandmother Peace to quiet
Down and sit by the warm fire,
For there was a story to be told
On that cold December night,
Of Preshious and Odatious and about
Their love and suffering and desire.
When Grandmother Peace knew she
Had the attention of the whole village,
Of every mortal living by breathing
And not just the children of Green,
She thus began the tale of those two
Souls who had lived centuries before
In an age of strife, both having sparkling beauty
For pure and sincere they had been.
T'was the third and final year of the *Awful War*
That the pretty Preshious was born
As the first child of a soldier and his wife
Only to be orphaned on her maiden day,
While across the rain starved street
Sat hiding, Odatious the four year old
Child of a dead prostitute with a ghastly

Stare, see a soldier and a lady burn like a stack of hay.
It was the villainous ruler Tyrant, of the
Kingdom of Greed who had invaded the village
Of Green among scores of others
To emerge as the supreme power,
And it was Tyrant and his army of
Greedians who had done away with every single
Life on the way to glory, to doom, making
Anyone left behind bear hell's shower.
Miraculous it be, that Preshious was
Not hurt under the burning roof, but the zero
Day old child was crying out in fright,
When someone ran to her and took her,
As it was Odatious, who lay hiding under a wagon
Saw Tyrant move away and slowly came out,
Shivering on seeing a fiery sight, rushed on
Hearing a baby's cry, into that very shelter.
The hopelessness spread like a paper caught by the wind
Tossing and turning every man's and woman's
Soul, tearing them apart, crushing them to
Powder as the villages finally fell to defeat,
As Green, Tree, Water and all the other
Villages had nothing to fight with, against
Tyrant of Greed who stamped out
Opposing factions with his fatty feat.
Not knowing what had ended, or what had
Commenced, Odatious ran with Preshious to

The pit of Slum where he lived now, that he knew
Even King Tyrant would not dream to capture,
For it was a place filled with people who didn't
Look like the *normal* kind, who had no heart
Or mind like the *normal* kind, and who lived
With abnormalities and bend to low stature.
To such a place, came Odatious with the
Little Preshious and straight he went to the hut
Of Mother Earth, the woman he and all in
Slum loved and revered,
For when the rest of the *normal* kind
Spat, shunned, hurled stones, thrashed,
And insulted them at the very sight,
Mother Earth gave the warmth they deserved.
When Odatious finished his story as the baby child
Lay with comfort in the arms of Mother Earth,
She turned to look at the baby who smiled a
Toothless smile and called her by Preshious, the name,
Which echoed into the heart of the slum
And the heart of Odatious, as this very girl
Brought magic and happiness into Slum as she
Grew from a baby to a girl to a jasmine of a dame.
Fifteen years passed, with the people of the
Villages suffering under the wrath of Tyrant
With all the produce going to him
And all allegiance was garnered by him,
To fight more, wreck more and

Lives were lost, wars were won when
Tyrant faced his first defeat as he came
Against the mighty Queen Ego of Kingdom Dim.
The war fought between Tyrant and Ego
Was massive and fierce, as even the gods
Came out to see the war unfurling on the
Mortal ground knee deep with blood,
But as is when we realize our folly in the
Midst of what we deem correct, Tyrant
Understood that he was wrong in paining
The innocent people, and fell with a thud.
Queen Ego's unnatural strength had opened
Tyrant's eyes to make him see how much
His own men despised him even as they lay
To die alongside Tyrant,
And realizing the gravity of his crime
The almighty ruler, up till half an hour ago,
Dropped his sword and raised his head to
The heaven, crying, the once greedy giant.
The long, sharp and heavy steel sword
Of Queen Ego pierced through Tyrant's
Armour and skin and cut through the heart
Of the heartless heart regained man,
Sending Tyrant to the ground like a felled
Tree, with the dust from the ground rising to
The air cleared away by Ego, whose smirk
Suggested what she will do, and can.

In those very fifteen years Preshious
Grew up into a fine young woman prized
And adored by all for her kindness and skills
And secretly craved by a man named Love,
And Odatious grew into a strong and meek lad
Respected for his strength of mind and will
Of the hands, for he too was adored and loved
By all and secretly craved by a girl named Dove.
For what purpose did the man named Love
And the girl named Dove secretly crave for that
Person of the opposite kind the people
Couldn't make sense of,
For the whole of Slum knew that Love and
Dove were but Odatious and Preshious
Who had given themselves to each other
But declined from public display and show off.
Though the life in Slum was hard to live
And many suffered from pain and agony,
Preshious and Odatious were always there
To sooth those poor souls each with a song,
And through the constant love and care
The couple spread a blanket of warmth
Across Slum that all mortals of that dirty
Pit began to feel alive, young and strong.
Thus, Slum a neglected piece of no man's land
For many years, began to rebuild and reform
Itself with the renewed energy and hope

That the people had been fed and filled,
With many turning to farming and many
Turning to building, many into the arts
And many into clothing, many into medicine
And many into education, that in all thrilled.
For education opened new vistas to the
Children enabling them to think and act
Better, to live and behave better
For it was the job taken up by Preshious,
But a foresight about neighbouring
Villages and kingdoms grow with spite
Over Slum's development, made the
Making of an army necessary, obvious.
Who else was the natural choice
To teach the men of Slum the
Art of making weapons and to fight
With courage and a heart,
As Odatious himself was assigned
The task of it all, and though about
Warfare he had no formal knowledge
His diligence shook every man with a start.
While the young of Slum came running
To Preshious every morning to learn,
She would take them to Mother Earth's
Prized Knowledge and Freedom tree,
That had a million leaves and a topic on
Each leaf which could be plucked,

Read and learnt, while another *topic* leaf
Would sprout there, on the count of three.
The army slowly started to form under
The able leadership of Odatious and gentle
Guidance from Mother Earth, who knew
Too well that war was soon to come,
And all that had to done, had to be done
With speed, care and dedication
As Mother Earth now knew that Queen Ego
Had started, with volcanic anger, to Slum.
The march towards Slum was with
An army thrice of which Ego used
For taking down King Tyrant
As beckoned over a sip of tea,
Were two beings with soldiers immense
Who, along with the Queen commanded
With wild pleasure the universe of man,
Lady Jealous and General Envy.
Beauty and love were treasures of
Lady Jealous and her recipes for luring
Men of beautiful wives, disowning
Them once her need was fulfilled,
That realizing those very recipes
Were with Preshious too, with her soul
Pledged to Odatious, entice him with joy
Was her plan and have his woman killed.
Speed of light, strength of a dozen lions,

Splendour of a white horse, sickly in crimes
To attractive women were all that was
General Envy the mad pilferer,
Who howled only one man of might need
Live, hearing the deeds of Odatious
And longed to see the divine Preshious
To distort and destroy, both him and her.
Thus equipped with two mighty
Warriors and their indestructible armies,
Queen Ego marched towards the pit now
Hailed as a burgeoning kingdom,
Which Ego would thwart at any cost
For her own Kingdom of Dim was despised
Despite her efforts to gain for her land
Anything worthy or credible as Slum.
Preshious and Odatious had hurt Queen
Ego's pride beyond repair and they were
Along with the people of Slum, going
To be tormented by her swords and arrows,
And they would all be destroyed and shall
Another victory be written, history created
For such were the ruminations of that
Inglorious being, marching to her own gallows.
Word arrived that Queen Ego would
Reach the outskirts of Slum in two days' time
Which made everyone hasten their duties
Assigned by Odatious who worked with honour,

To ensure a prosperous future, a future rid of
Ego, envy and jealousy with his dear Preshious
To the children of that heavenly pit
Making them, each a happy *smile* donor.
In between of all the work to be made,
Preshious and Odatious escaped into
The woods one night, to remain in each
Other's arms for a few moments,
For weeks of preparation and teaching
Had given them no time to speak, no
Time to see and both were within,
Being subject to various torments.
It was an unusually cold night with
Rain pouring, a mild grace in it,
Dampening the woods and leaves
But sharpening the feeling,
Of that gay couple as they finally
Reached their favourite rest point
And kissed a perpetual kiss, so
Dramatic and medicinal, it's healing.
The fifteen years of their lives since
Preshious's arrival played through the
Eyes of Love and Dove, the first moments
Of romance in the air for the boy,
That slowly paved way into the heart
Of that girl who was saved by him, who
In turn saved him from the abyss of gluttony

As she was tender, selfless and a tad coy.
Now the war declared on Slum, was
A war on Preshious and Odatious as well
As Lady jealous had spat out those ill
Words that pained Preshious,
Who thought of existence without
Odatious but a mere farce, an orphaned
Being from start destined to remain
No one's, in this world, so ravenous.
So was Odatious in doubt, of his
Strength to lead against General Envy
Who had roared he would prevail
And not Odatious, in the end,
Who then wouldn't be there to
Protect his Preshious and his land
That he lost faith in the midst of
What he couldn't comprehend.
Both lovers submerged in doubt
And agony, wet in tears from their
Eyes looked at each other, smiled and
Kissed slowly again with each caress,
Giving the additional vigour to face
The danger coming to them, and the
Lock of the lips and joined souls giving
Rise to inner might, to control and harness.
All was set and all was ready for
The people of Slum, the obnoxious

To the *normal* kind, to tackle it out,
And to create history, to write songs,
For now Slum faced a disposition so
Unique, so grave, so senseless such as
A war yet willing to go through it and
Fight, as they sounded their gongs.
As the sun retired down the horizon
The people of Slum gathered along with
Mother Earth to pray for victory and peace
And then the Mother took out two rings,
With a radiant smile on her face that
Realization dawned upon the people
That Dove and Love were to marry on
That moonlit, cold December evening.
Dressed in white with smiles on their lips
And sadness in their bosoms, the man and
Woman of the hour walked up to Mother
Earth as they were bestowed with blessings,
By every man, woman, child, every insect,
Every blade of grass and every flower and
As tears rolled down Preshious's eyes
On the fingers were placed the olive leaved rings.
The spies, shivering with fright, arrived
At the camp of Ego, stationed not far
From Slum with the news of the marriage
Between Preshious and Odatious,
Which ignited the fire in the three monsters

That the massive armies were called
Upon and ordered to attack Slum that
Very moment, and burn it to ashes.
The celebrations in the pit of Slum
Were at the peak with everyone dancing
And laughing to the music played out
As it was right then a time to rest,
To unwind from the arduous war
Preparations that had left all with
Tired bodies but not withered minds
And so they revelled, with delight and jest.
The armies of the dark side thundered
Their way to Slum with swords, arrows and
Fireballs and with hearts filled to the brim
With prejudice and anger and hate,
For they marked their presence at the
Enemy's yard by hurling a mammoth
Fireball one after the other, in a sum of
Four that shattered the walls and the city gate.
Happiness took no time to turn to fright
As the civilians of Slum rushed to safety,
Creating a stampede that crushed many
Young and killed the feeble and old,
With Preshious and Odatious standing
With hairs on end and terror in their
Eyes as they witnessed the carnage
Of their beloved home in that cold.

Mother Earth commanded Odatious and
Preshious to take with them the people
Who had the strength to fight and do
What they could till they fell,
And heading the words of the saintly
Mother the newlywed couple parted ways
With a divine smile and a secret in their
Eyes that the Mother knew, but wouldn't tell.
It was destruction of a magnitude never
Before seen that the gentle hearted
People of Slum couldn't bear the sight
Of their city's death that they all stood,
To fight the evil Queen Ego, Lady Jealous
And General Envy who had arrived at the
Very moment to see that haven crumble
And to wipe out those fighters as they could.
The task of ridding those common
People were an easy task for the three
Devils, that Queen Ego soon proposed she would
Have it out with Mother Earth,
While Lady Jealous go after Odatious
And General Envy after Preshious
Which was agreed upon and terror
Struck on the way, with mirth.
As Queen Ego arrived at the Tree of
Knowledge and Freedom she was welcomed
By bodies charred by fire with an old woman's,

Mother Earth's too, who had to witness,
The tree being fervently cut with Queen
Ego happily allowing Mother to watch the sight
With tears and an immovable body that
She closed her eyes with sickness.
The men who fought alongside Preshious
All fell with their bodies spilling out
Blood and General Envy remained hungry
For Odatious's Dove and not more for fight,
That with every rotten tread that malicious
Man slowly came towards the wounded,
Fallen, immobile Preshious and crouched towards
Her as she closed her eyes with all her might.
Odatious and his men could stand the onslaught
Not much longer, and the men slowly fell
To the ground with parts separated, dead
And Lady Jealous ready to fulfil her want,
Of tainting the young and divine Love of
Preshious, broke every bone of that soul
And leaned down to Odatious who with eyes
Closed, prayed for freedom from the taunt.
The tree that had given immense joy fell
Along with the destruction of that angelic
City and its beautiful citizens, Mother Earth,
Preshious, Odatious and its' animals and flowers,
And Queen Ego emerged victorious as
She stood amidst the gigantic fire, which

Aptly symbolised her unfulfilling greed,
Her pride and arrogance, two inseparable lovers.
Thus Slum was lost for those poor souls
Living in that pit who knew nothing of war
And nothing of illicit thoughts who in the
End died alongside their land,
While Slum was won, counted as the
Greatest victory of the Queen and her
Lady and General who knew nothing of
Care and love and lending a helping hand.
The victory over Slum, that dirty pit
As it was called till some time ago was
Momentous as no other King or Queen
From the past had thoughts club,
To bring Slum under their wings
Or either try to, and here Ego stood
With full flare as her armies paid her
Rich tributes over this thumping drub.
Queen Ego, Lady Jealous and General
Envy now raised their swords to the
Heavens and declared themselves
Equal to, no, above the Supreme,
As their egotism took them to newer
Heights giving them a sense of
Infallibility that one such would feel
Before becoming history's despicable dream.
Tolerance had reached the zenith, and

The climate over the decimated Slum turned
With gigantic ferocity, as heavy black
Clouds swirled like vultures hovering,
The three devils and their armies
And as they all stood now feeling miniscule
In front of nature, a roar of thunder and
A bolt of lightning sending all cowering.
As Preshious and Odatious had laid to
Die in two corners of Slum, they had closed
Their eyes and prayed to the Almighty
About their small dream and desire,
Which was felt by the wise Mother Earth
Who too joined the couple, married
On that ill fated day, and seeked for that
Blessing, till her last breath, from the sire.
Heavy rains lashed out onto the fire fed
Slum, washing all the blood and heat
Away, soothing the swollen ground and
As the villains stood aghast,
They saw with their naked eyes the
Souls of Slum, golden in colour, rise
From the bodies and fly to the sky
With Ego and her lot not to live a second past.
What King Tyrant felt the day he died
Might have struck upon the mighty Queen
Ego, that now she felt deserted and frail
And tired that she stopped moving,

Sensing all was lost that was thought
Won, and all that was loved was
Now vanishing into that sin filled
Air, her dreams gone, and Ego crying.
The end neared, as the dark shadows
That ruled the creation, saw cracks
Appear on the ground shaking so
Violently that hot fumes escaped out,
And the shaking turned into an
Earthquake that devoured and swallowed
All in its path that consumed Ego,
Jealous and Envy with a gargantuan shout.
The war between the people of Slum
And Queen Ego lasted for hours
With a bloody victory won by the
Side of the *normal* kind, a worthless gain,
But a much greater, more easier
Victory was the war won over Ego
By Nature who had had enough, said
Grandmother Peace, of the mortal pain.
The village of Green was now silent
As never before had they heard a
Story so grave yet gentle and true to
The heart that many had their eyes wet,
But what of the wish that was wished
Asked a young child to Grandmother
Peace who smiled and stood up saying

That she would tell as all were ready and set.
While they lay to die, Preshious and
Odatious had only one wish, that to live
Together not alone, but with everyone of
Slum, as one family, together,
Which was whole heartedly supported by
Mother Earth who too joined to pray
For an eternal life for all the souls of
Slum, to fly free like a feather.
The golden souls were granted their wish,
Said Grandmother Peace, for look to the
Sky now dear ones and see, and as the people
Raised their heads to the sky they saw,
Flying through the celestial, star studded
Space, a group of golden meteors, showering
Their way across the dark blue atmosphere
Which was looked upon with awe.
Every eye of Green was now being filled with
That enchanting visual sight and adding
To the beauty was a mild scented cold wind
Which reminded the people of *one* reality,
That everyone screamed out in joy,
In wonder, as they saw towards the end
Of the meteor shower two elegant
Meteors joined in the middle, for eternity.
Mother's meteors was the name given
For that stunning heavenly feast which

Passed the humankind every ten years
On that cold December night,
Said Grandmother Peace who had
Seen Mother's meteors eight times
Before and was happy to show her
Baby children this extravagant sight,
Tomorrow my children we shall go
To the Knowledge and Freedom Tree
That has witnessed Mother's meteors
Fifty times Grandmother added,
But does the tree exist asked a child
Enthusiastically, for which the reply came
That neither Knowledge nor Freedom or
Mother Earth's tree would get faded.
And so the children and their parents
Slept that night, that very night that
Had seen the marriage of Love and Dove
And their fight for life with Queen Ego,
And the children and their parents slept
With inner calmness alongside Grand-
Mother Peace who had recited to them
All a message for life, never to let go.
The villagers of Green learnt that
It was goodness that finally paid
And not greed and pride and
Gait and arrogance,
For each human life was a gift

From the heaven to spread joy,
Love and care and to be remembered
For propagating a divine fragrance.
Thus, the children, the parents, and
Grandmother Peace of Village Green paid
Homage to those brave souls who gave
Freedom to these crushed villages,
Who under Queen Ego had suffered
Plenty, and remembering the value of
What they had received and what they
Learnt, would be their fuel for coming ages.
The villagers of Green thanked the Almighty
For the blessings given to them, for the food
And shelter, for their humble lives and
Prayed they remain steadfast and courageous,
But when everyone closed their eyes
To sleep, they all were overwhelmed by that
Incorruptible human story, as told by Grand-
Mother Peace, of Preshious and Odatious.

Also By The Author

1. LIFE AND TIMES IN KOLAAZHAM PART 1

ISBN: 9781638324560

2. KOODUMBOL IMBAM ഒരു തിരക്കഥ

ISBN: 9781685384791

(BOTH BOOKS ARE AVAILABLE ON AMAZON AND NOTIONPRESS)

9 798885 695213

Printed by Libri Plureos GmbH in Hamburg, Germany